How to not ruin your life

The one book every 16 year old must read

Copyright @2023 Quentin Garantino. All rights reserved.
How to not ruin your life

Quentin Garantino
c/o AutorenServices.de
Birkenallee 24
36037 Fulda
Germany

ISBN: 9798866174850
Imprint: Independently published

Disclaimer:

The information presented in this book is for informational purposes only and is not intended to replace professional advice. The author and the publisher do not guarantee the accuracy, completeness, or timeliness of the provided information. Any actions taken based on the information contained in this book are at your own risk. It is recommended to consult a specialist or an appropriate professional to address specific questions or issues, especially when in doubt.

For my parents

Contents

1.) Introduction. _____ 7
2.) Never jump from the balcony into the hotel pool. _____ 13
3.) In a fight, never allow yourself to be picked up _____ 23
4.) Why you shouldn't brand yourself with a branding iron _____ 31
5.) Why you shouldn't race on a motorcycle_____ 37
6.) Take cover when blowing things up _____ 41
7.) Why you should pay special attention to trees when skiing _____ 45
8.) Don't buy unnecessary things on credit _____ 49
9.) Don't do crazy tricks on a trampoline_____ 53
10.) Why you shouldn't jump out of moving trains or cars _____ 57
11.) Don't risk your life for a cool selfi. _____ 61
12.) Stay away from the bowling pinsetter _____ 65
13.) Why you shouldn't even start smoking _____ 69
14.) Why you shouldn't climb on a pool cover_____ 75
15.) Why you should never put your feet up as a passenger _____ 79
16.) Always have the headrest behind your head in the car _____ 83
17.) Always put your smartphone in the glove box_____ 85
18.) Why you should never go near small dams or rapids _____ 91
19.) Why you shouldn't listen to music loudly _____ 97
20.) Never fall asleep outside drunk in winter_____ 101
21.) Never drink a whole bottle of hard alcohol in one go_____ 105
22.) Never put a New Year's Eve firecrackers in your mouth _____ 111
23.) Don't ruin your Life!_____ 115

1.)

Introduction and why you shouldn't light fireworks out of your ass.

Stupidity level: 8/10

Risk level: 8/10

It was New Year's Eve and Dan, Andy and Josh had decided to spend the last night of the year together. They had spent the day preparing for the upcoming party, with music, beer and delicious food. By 10 p.m. they were already in the best party mood and slightly drunk. The friends had a great time together, sharing stories from their past and laughing at the funniest anecdotes. As the clock approached midnight, the anticipation and alcohol levels continued to rise. The prospect of the New Year's Eve party they planned to attend later promised a lot of fun and good memories.

But then, in the midst of their exuberant mood and spurred on by a few more drinks, Josh came up with the stupidest idea of his life so far. He thought it would be a brilliant idea to jam a New Year's Eve rocket into his ass cheeks, lie down on the grass and let the rocket launch from there. His friends Dan and Andy were thrilled by this fascinating inspiration. Andy immediately offered his services as a cameraman.

The friends decided to give it a try without thinking about how dangerous and nonsensical the idea actually was. Josh lay down on the grass, pulled his pants down a bit and stuck a rocket between his bottoms. The other two stood excitedly and cheered Josh on as he ignited the rocket.

In his mind, the rocket would just fly from his ass straight into the sky and explode with a loud bang. His friends would cheer him on, and probably the entire neighborhood would congratulate him on his heroic act. Girls also like guys who heroically light rockets out of their asses. His thought process was something like that.

But the reality was different. First of all, the firwork did not take off immediately, but instead gave off a lot of fire and sparks. This converted flamethrower was now aimed directly at Josh's rear end. And not just for a short moment, but for 7 eternally long seconds. As Josh screamed in pain and writhed around on the lawn, the rocket finally exploded with a loud bang.

Dan and Andy laughed so loudly that they attracted the attention of other revelers on the street. Nobody knew yet that they would spend New Year's Eve together in the hospital. This rarely stupid idea is actually done more often than you think. Apparently every year a few teenagers come up with the brilliant idea of launching a rocket out of their asses. In fact, such a story is the reason for this book. After reading a Reddit post with such an action, I became aware of a longer comment:

„Former 6 year surgical RN now in a different specialty. You're in for a long, painful recovery following a serious wound or burn near your "Peri area". Think of how often you visit the bathroom and then imagine you have a third degree burn down there. It's devastating every single time.

If really bad, he will be in the burn unit and levels of care to follow for months if not north of a year. Job, relationships, and any semblance of normalcy immediately disrupted. Burns are monumentally painful, and he will be sedated heavily until substantial healing begins. He will develop tolerance and possibly become addicted to the potent opiates, but they're the best way we currently know how to cope with that level of pain short of a spinal or other nerve block which are also options. Medicating at that level can also be very expensive, I've seen ICU patients with over $5,000 a day in IV medication costs alone, 7 days a week, not including any other charges for the room, MDs, nursing and ancillary staff, and supplies for starters.

Staff may have to place a fecal catheter less than a foot up his anus to drain his feces so they don't contaminate his burn wounds. His poo goes into a bag and has to be emptied and measured as they'll give him laxatives to loosen and prevent clogged drain lines. Fecal contamination generally results in rapid infection, and peri wounds are at an extreme risk for MRSA and flesh eating bacterial infections. I've seen entire legs removed to combat severe peri, groin, or hip joint infections. This is usually following weeks or months of previous failed treatments, but still. We can work wonders until we can't, and even then there's always amputation.

If he needs skin grafts, they can be sourced from a human or large mammal cadaver like cows and pigs. I've also seen skin grafts harvested from the front of a patient's thigh and reattached to the burn area (abdomen). The grafts aren't actually solid strips of skin, rather, they are more like tight lace with repeated spaces between skin making the graft look like a Kleenex with several hundred small oval shaped holes in it. These spaces make it easier for the graft adhere and conform to the wound bed.

The surgeon uses a specialized skin shaver that's handheld, covered in a sterile barrier with single use blades, very similar to deli counter meat slicers but on a smaller more specialized scale. So not only did the patient have a burn on her abdomen, but a very unusual, superficial wound on her right thigh that looked liked like we had lightly crushed her leg with a cheese grater. The primary benefit of harvesting skin grafts from ourselves is we (usually) don't reject ourselves, and rejection is the biggest complication accompanying foreign body transplants.

He'll also need to lay on his stomach throughout this whole ordeal due to the location of the burn and subsequent wound. Imagine months lying on your stomach in 6-11/10 pain. It's a personal living hell. Diet will also be bland as fuck when he's actually allowed to eat again. Social and professional life obliterated. This could set him back years and give him decades of PTSD.

He should consider himself "good" when he can sit and shit without bleeding out or collapsing in pain. On the even shittier side, this, or whatever transpires for this poor guy could easily kill or disable him for life. This could go in a thousand directions for him, and 880 of them result in the quality of his life being worse than it was prior to the Incident.

If his burn is bad enough and he really does require months of care, his bill from arrival at the ER to discharge from outpatient rehab and specialty care will easily exceed 1 million in the US. Two million would push it, but also not shock me either. I'd bet on 1.2-1.5M if he's inpatient for 2.5 months and receiving follow up care for 1.5 years. Overall, don't fucking do this. If you drink around fireworks you need a sober or not shitty friend who won't let you do this kind of *stupid shit. We can all learn from these videos even though were not the dumbass with the firework up his ass."*

Admittedly, it never occurred to me to stick a rocket up my ass, but I can understand the thought process. Something like this could definitely have happened in my circle of friends when I was growing up. Almost a sure thing, provided there is enough alcohol and rockets. Luckily nothing happened to me. If I had read this comment beforehand, I would categorically reject such nonsense. At the same time, this comment is the reason why I wrote this book.

There are so many times when teenagers carelessly underestimate the risk of crazy actions and thereby jeopardize their future. These extraordinary situations are often so absurd that they do not appear in any serious guidebook. In any case, in school we are not taught the catastrophic consequences that stupid decisions can have. Normally common sense protects us from this, but for many teenagers this seems to be temporarily suspended.

What you may not know as a teenager is that your brain continues to develop, and it isn't until around age 25 that it truly matures. That means. that you are currently most likely overestimating your own abilities and generally underestimating risks. For every 20 videos of daredevils cavorting on high scaffolding, there is at least one who didn't survive.

If this book has fallen into your hands, you are part of the target group that probably needs it urgently. You probably got it as a gift from someone who is convinced that you will one day dig your own grave through your stupid actions. It is designed in such a way that it first describes a seemingly entertaining situation and then shows the harsh consequences in a brutal and realistic way - with the aim of keeping you away from such actions in the future.

This book serves as a guide and safety net to protect you from the idiotic situations that reckless teenagers find themselves in every year. Each of these situations has the potential to ruin the rest of your life in an instant with one bad decision.

"How to not ruin your life" is certainly not a literary masterpiece, but it protects your life.

So if you or your friends ever get the idea to do something crazy, remember the following stories and you'll get through the next few years unscathed.

2.)

Why you shouldn't jump from the balcony into the hotel pool.

Stupidity level: 8/10
Risk level: 9/10

Jonas and his friends had treated themselves to an exciting break from everyday life and traveled together to a chic hotel in a sunny holiday destination. The sixth floor offered a breathtaking view of the azure sea, and the friends shared a spacious hotel room. They had been exploring for days, enjoying the nightlife and delicious local cuisine.

Before the trip, they had joked about jumping from the balcony into the hotel pool. But now, with alcohol in his blood, the idea seemed more tempting than ever. Jonas found himself on the balcony of the sixth floor, looking at the pool, which was three meters from the hotel wall. The thought of the jump filled him with both excitement and fear. The pool was relatively close, about three meters away, but it was still a considerable distance that Jonas would have to overcome.

"That would be the stunt of my life," he thought. "The memory of this journey that will never bore us." But at the same time fear gnawed at him. What if he couldn't jump the full three meters? But it looks very easy from up here."

Max, who was a little more level-headed, tried to dissuade Jonas from the idea. "Jonas, that's crazy. What if you get hurt? This is the dumbest idea you've ever had"

Lucas and Timo, on the other hand, continued to heat up the mood. "Come on, if you jump, we'll jump too".

Jonas stood on the balcony, the railing in front of him. His heart was racing and he knew he had to make a serious decision. The mix of thrill, alcohol and excitement weighed heavily on him. At this crucial moment he had to ask himself whether he was really ready to take the risk and jump from that balcony. However, inside he already knew the answer. Jumping from the balcony was the first thing that came to his mind since arriving in the hotel room and the thought never left his mind. He knew he would jump.

Jonas stood at the edge of the balcony, his friends cheering him on, the alcohol dulling his senses. With one last deep breath and a nervous smile, he climbed onto the railing. But as he prepared to jump, he noticed that his legs were shaking. At the same time, he loved the adrenaline rush. He ignored the thought of the possible consequences.

He hesitated a moment too long. When he finally jumped out, it all happened too quickly. Jonas' feet didn't quite hit the edge of the balcony and he slipped slightly. At that moment he realized his mistake, but it was already too late.

In a split second, as he floated in the air and headed toward the pool, Jonas wished he could turn back time. His heart was racing and the dizziness of the altitude had turned into a real nightmare. He tried desperately to coordinate his legs and correct his fall, but his efforts seemed futile. Everything happened in slow motion.

Jonas' body hit the hard edge of the pool and a sharp pain shot through his back. The impact was so intense that he held his breath for a moment and was in danger of losing consciousness. But he fought against the darkness that seemed to be spreading in his eyes.

Jonas lay at the edge of the pool with his eyes closed, his body riddled with pain. His friends immediately recognized the seriousness of the situation and called an ambulance. When the paramedics arrived and carefully examined Jonas, it quickly became clear that this careless jump from the balcony would have devastating consequences. Jonas suffered serious injuries when he hit the edge of the pool. In addition to a severe concussion and a cut on his forehead that required stitches, he suffered serious injuries to his spine. Doctors explained to his friends that Jonas was now a paraplegic, meaning he would no longer have control of his legs and could require support for life.

Jonas' friends were devastated when they heard the sad news. The fun and excitement they wanted to experience on their journey had turned into a painful nightmare that had changed Jonas' life forever. Her recklessness and impulsive decisions had tragic consequences.

Conclusion:

Don't jump lightly, be it from a balcony or from a cliff with unsteady ground. The risk of ruining your life is disproportionate to the excitement you get from the jump. After a year, your jump will be long forgotten, but you will have to bear the consequences of a wrong landing for the rest of your life.

3.)

In a fight, never allow yourself to be picked up and never lift anyone up!

Stupidity level: 6/10
Risk level: 7/10

Henry and Dennis have been best friends since childhood. Not only did they share the same birthday, but they also shared the same interests and passions. One day they received an invitation to a birthday party from their mutual friend, Chris. The party was supposed to take place in a chic bar in the city center, and the two friends' anticipation knew no bounds.

The night of the party, Henry and Dennis arrived early to make sure they got a good spot near the bar. The music was loud and the atmosphere was exuberant. The two friends enjoyed the company of the other guests, drank a few cocktails and laughed at old stories.

But the later the evening got, the more alcohol flowed and the mood began to change. A group of young men who had clearly had too much to drink began misbehaving. They stumbled around, pushing people and insulting guests. Henry and Dennis tried to ignore the situation and concentrate on their own conversation.

However, at some point everything went wrong. Henry had already drunk more than usual that evening and was feeling more confident than usual. One of the drunk men stumbled straight towards Henry and accidentally spilled his drink down his shirt. Henry, who was usually a patient person, couldn't help himself at that moment and reacted angrily. "What the hell are you doing here?" he shouted to the man.

Dennis, who immediately recognized the situation, tried to calm Henry down and defuse the conflict. But the drunken men were now out of control and began to provoke the boys. It didn't take long for the situation to escalate and partygoers began to form a circle around the two groups.

Henry and Dennis knew they couldn't hold back any longer. They had no intention of using violence, but the drunken men left them no choice. A wild fistfight broke out as the other partygoers looked on in shock.

Henry and Dennis, who had known each other well since childhood and were normally peaceful, suddenly found themselves involved in an unexpected argument. The loud bangs and shouting carried over the music and the bar atmosphere turned into chaos and uncertainty.

Despite their determination not to use violence, the boys defended themselves as best they could. The surrounding guests were shocked by the sudden violence and didn't know how to react. Some shouted for help while others tried to call the police.

Henry let himself be carried away by his anger and countered the wild blows that rained down on him. His hands flew in quick movements to block blows while keeping a clear head. Meanwhile, Dennis tried to calm the situation and blocked the drunken men's attacks as best he could.

Suddenly Henry and one of the drunken men got into a heated argument. The two wrestled and tried to take each other down. Henry fought with all his strength and determination to maintain control of the situation. His muscles tensed and his expression was one of determination.

With a last desperate gasp, Henry managed to lift the drunken man up and hold him in the air for a brief moment. The guests in the bar looked on in amazement as Henry lifted his opponent into the air. He then slammed the attacker headfirst onto the ground.

A loud screech went through the room. The other opponents stood back and waited for the situation to unfold. Her friend didn't move. His head was in a strange tilted position. Two spectators immediately threw themselves between Henry and the attacker lying on the ground. Someone else checked the attacker's pulse.

He is dead.

Henry's face suddenly turned pale.

He had just killed someone.

He knew in that moment that his life would never be the same again. The attacker's friends pushed the spectators aside and attacket Henry. After what felt like an eternity and two lost teeth, spectators were able to tear the attackers away from him. He couldn't believe what had happened in the last five minutes.

He had just killed someone and ruined his own life at the same time.

Police arrived at the scene and took Henry into custody. The investigation concluded that he had indeed acted in self-defense, but that didn't mean he would get off scot-free. The laws in his region were strict, and prosecutors decided to press charges against him.

He was taken to court and the trial dragged on for months. The legal costs piled up, and Henry had to hire a lawyer he could barely afford. Public opinion was against him and the media reported extensively on the case.

Ultimately, he was found guilty, even if he had acted in self-defense. He was sentenced to a long prison sentence that changed his life forever. The court costs and fines he had to pay drove him to financial ruin.

In prison, he struggled daily with the memories of his crime. He couldn't believe how his life had gone down the drain so quickly. He was isolated from his family and friends and found no comfort in his situation.

The years passed, but Henry could never really come to terms with the crime. The psychological consequences of his actions haunted him day and night. His future was bleak and he couldn't imagine how he would ever live a normal life again.

Conclusion:

Reality differs significantly from a feature film. In movies, it can seem like someone will just pass out if you hit them in the face. But in reality the situation is far more dangerous. There is a high chance that a person will be seriously injured or even killed by a punch to the face alone, especially if you have significantly more mass than your opponent. Likewise, if your opponent falls unconscious on the asphalt, it can end up fatal or cause serious injury much quicker than you think.

If you even pick someone up and throw them to the ground with force, the likelihood that your opponent will suffer serious spinal injuries or even die increases exponentially. In sports like wrestling, such holds are strictly forbidden for good reason and legally such a throw is often considered attempted homicide. So under no circumstances throw your opponent to the ground!

At the same time, you should do everything in your power not to be lifted yourself. Once you're in the air, you lose your footing and it becomes extremely difficult to defend yourself. Do everything in your power to prevent this. It's best to avoid all fights right away.

4.)

Why you shouldn't brand yourself with a branding iron.

Stupidity level: 9/10

Risk level: 9/10

The whiskey had had its effect on the boys. Tim, Adam and Alex had met at Alex's father's farm and wanted to have a drink before going to the graduation party in the neighborhood. The boys had known each other for years and had grown up in their small town. They had all graduated college and were about to make big changes in their lives. Each of them knew that their paths would soon be very different.

That evening the air was heavy with the heat of summer. The drinks were already flowing freely and the atmosphere was exuberant. Behind the farm they sat around the campfire and started talking about their future plans. Alex had always dreamed of taking over his father's farm and building a successful farming business. Tim wanted to travel the world and have adventures, while Adam dreamed of a career as a professional athlete.

Leaning in the corner was an old branding iron that Alex's father usually used for his cows. It was rusty and old, but it somehow fascinated the boys. They had seen it many times before when they hung out here, but this night it seemed to have a special appeal.

After a few more drinks and the test of courage to see who could hold their hand over the fire longer, Tim suddenly came up with the glorious idea: "Let's get a brand! It stays forever and is cooler than any tattoo. That will seal our friendship, before we all go out into the world." The idea was immediately met with enthusiasm. What could be so bad about it? The cows get one all the time. Adam volunteered first and took off his shirt. They wanted the brand to be somewhere where it wouldn't be immediately visible, so they chose the chest. Tim put the brand in the fire and warmed it up while Alex pulled out his smartphone and shot a video.

"This will be a hit!" As the brand glowed more and more, Adam became more and more nervous and began to have doubts. Was that really a good idea? Another sip of whiskey. "Fuck yes it is!" And if something goes wrong, I have a bottle of water next to me, he thought. "And action!" was all he heard before Tim took the branding iron and slowly pressed it against his chest.

Adam didn't know at that moment that within a minute he had ruined his life because of a stupid idea. They had not considered that humans are not cattle and that our bodies are structured significantly differently. Let's look at what exactly happens:

The brand has a temperature of approximately 1292 to 1832 degrees Fahrenheit (700-1000 degrees Celsius) and will immediately cause third degree burns. In contrast to cattle skin and the thick layers of fat underneath, humans only have very thin skin.

The impact of a very hot object on the breast results in extreme thermal stress on the skin and underlying tissue. It undoubtedly causes severe third degree burns:

The heat of the fire penetrated his flesh, causing severe burns with extreme stress on the skin and underlying tissues. These burns were third degree, meaning they had penetrated all layers of skin down to the muscle. In third-degree burns, not only the top layer of skin (epidermis) is affected, but also the layers of skin underneath (dermis and subcutis).

For a brief moment, Adam will feel extreme pain, but it will quickly subside. The branding iron penetrated his skin so far that the heat destroyed the nerve endings in the affected area. At this moment, Adam can no longer feel pain in his chest. At the same time, Adam experiences a shock reaction. The body can respond to the stress of the injury by lowering blood pressure and increasing heart rate. This can cause confusion, weakness, rapid heartbeat, and other symptoms.

Since human skin is much thinner than that of cattle, the branding iron slides not only through the layers of skin, but also through the fatty tissue and muscles. These are now forever destroyed in his chest.

When Tim loosens the branding iron, the boys realize they've made a huge mistake. The hole in Adam's chest is more than a centimeters deep and smells of burnt flesh. It looks unreal as you can see right into Adam's chest and the burnt flesh is visible around the edges. Just two seconds were enough to burn a deep hole. Another second longer and the iron would have burned all the way to Adam's bones.

Only when Adam sees the horrified faces of Tim and Alex does he realize the damage he has done to himself. Adam is immediately taken to the hospital and has to spend the next few days there. His wound is so deep that he was lucky to escape with his life.

The body responds to the burn with an inflammatory response that manifests itself as swelling, redness, and pain as immune cells rush to the injured area to fight infection and repair tissue. Third-degree burns can significantly compromise the skin barrier, increasing the risk of infection. The open wound is susceptible to bacteria and other pathogens. One reason why doctor's visits have become normal for Adam lately.

While his other friends start exciting new phases in their lives, Adam has to carefully disinfect and clean his wound every day. Due to the severe muscle injury, many movements that strain the chest muscles cause him considerable difficulty. In addition, any form of bodybuilding proves to be pointless for him, as his muscles are not only destroyed, but can no longer grow back. In any case, he will only be able to practice sports with extreme caution in the coming years. The cost of his hospital treatment has quickly risen exponentially, so Adam will be paying it off for many years to come.

Conclusion:

It can be said that a self-made brand on the body will definitely backfire. If you or a buddy of yours comes up with this stupid idea, remember Adam's story and just let it go.

5.)

Why you shouldn't race on a motorcycle.

Stupidity level: 5/10

Risk level: 7/10

You may be wondering if a moral sermon is coming? I can understand that you don't want to jump off a hotel roof into a pool, but riding a motorcycle?

Yes, because riding a motorcycle is damn dangerous. Do you remember how I explained in the opening text that your brain is not yet as developed as an adult? This means you think you're making good decisions, but in reality you're often making pretty stupid ones. One of them is often motorcycling, because we all know: you wouldn't stick to the speed limit, otherwise they wouldn't have given you this book. So you often tend to make bad decisions or overestimate yourself in risky situations. You are not alone, as over 35% of motorcyclists who are fatally injured are under the age of 24.

In general, motorcyclists are four times more likely to have accidents than drivers on the same roads.

Are you perhaps thinking that these motorcyclists are simply not as capable as you and this can't happen to you? Most fatal accidents are not the fault of the motorcyclist, but of a car driver.

For one thing, you are much smaller and therefore less visible than a car. On the other hand, you will suffer completely different injuries.

Where a car crashes into another car and only results in fender damage, a motorcyclist can lose his life. The protection in a car is many times higher than on a motorcycle. You don't have the mass to protect you from a collision, nor do you have a seat belt. No, you just fly around and hope that nothing is in your path. Because if something is in your path, you will hit it at high speed and be smashed. No helmet or protective suit can protect you against a quick impact. This is the reason why almost every doctor in the hospital advises you not to ride a motorcycle.

Conclusion:

Choose a car instead. In a car you can transport more, listen to music better and even sleep in it. If you still can't help it, don't drive like a wild man and hope that the drivers do the same.

6.)

Take cover when blowing things up!

Stupidity level: 6/10

Risk level: 6/10

Jan and Timo had already arranged to meet on January 1st, the day after New Year's Eve. After an exciting New Year's Eve, they wanted to continue their partying spirit in a unique way. They had decided to blow up the old refrigerator from Jan's father's yard.

January 1st was cold and foggy, but that didn't stop the two friends from putting their plans into action. They met in the yard and Jan led Timo to an old refrigerator that was rusty and abandoned in a corner.

Together they started putting all of their leftover fireworks in the fridge. Rockets, fountains and several illegal firecrackers from Poland - they packed everything in. The two friends laughed at the bizarre idea and looked forward to the upcoming spectacle.

Once everything was ready, they took a few steps back to ignite the refrigerator at the same time. With big grins on their faces, they lit the fuse and hid behind a nearby tree, about 10 meters away. Certainly enough distance, Jan thought.

A deafening bang shook the area and the old refrigerator exploded in all directions. The unexpected explosion was far more spectacular than they had ever imagined. Tiny pieces of debris flew in all directions, unfortunately right into Jan's face. To be more precise, a tiny piece of metal flew right into Jan's eye. He screamed in pain. The particle was no larger than a grain of sand, but it had caused a lot of damage.

Jan screamed in pain and tried to open his eye, but he couldn't see anything. The friends immediately rushed to him and took him to the hospital.

There, doctors diagnosed a serious eye injury that had almost completely destroyed his right eye. Jan could only perceive light and shadow and could hardly see anything in this eye. The news came as a shock to him and left him feeling desperate and sad.

Doctors said they would do their best to save his sight, but there was no guarantee that his eye would ever function normally again. Jan underwent complicated eye surgery and began a long, painful recovery period.

Conclusion:

If you're going to blow things up, at least take adequate cover. Small pieces of debris often fly much further than you think and can cause major damage.

7.)

Why you should pay special attention to trees when skiing or snowboarding.

Stupidity level: 4/10

Risk level: 7/10

On a bright winter day in the mountains, Jonas and Adam went on an adventure together by pursuing their passion for snowboarding. The snow-covered landscape and cloudless sky promised a perfect day on the slopes. After they put on their snowboards, Jonas decided to take the lead while Adam followed.

With adrenaline in his veins, Jonas fell down the slope. Suddenly, while trying to avoid a tight curve, he lost control and fell headfirst into a dangerous tree pit, also known as a "treewell."

A treewell is a deep pit or depression around the trunk of a tree in deep snow. These depressions form when snow falls around the tree and becomes compacted, while the area beneath the tree becomes less compacted due to protection from snow. This results in the formation of a pit that is often deep and difficult to see.

Jonas found himself in a moment of frightening silence as he found himself stuck upside down in this snowy trap. He tried desperately to free himself, but the more he struggled, the deeper he sank into the snow. He realized he was in trouble and desperately needed Adam's help.

Meanwhile, Adam desperately searched for Jonas, who had apparently disappeared without a trace. He followed the tracks and paid attention to every unevenness in the snow. Minutes felt like hours as he searched for his friend. Finally, Adam spotted a snowboard sticking out of the snow. He immediately began digging his way to Jonas. Every second counted because Adam could run out of air at any time.

Finally, Jonas was able to dig a small hole around Adam's face, which was covered in snow, so that he could breathe again. Then he carefully and carefully dug it out completely.

Treewells can be extremely dangerous as they can trap anyone who falls into them, be they hikers, skiers or snowboarders. People who get caught in a treewell have difficulty extricating themselves because the snow around them can be very loose and deep. Many skiers and snowboarders have died a slow, dangerous death in a treewell.

Conclusion:

Never ski or snowboard alone and always look out for your companion. Always wear brightly colored clothing that is clearly visible. Pay attention to trees on your ski slope. A death trap could be waiting next to any one of them.

8.)

Don't buy unnecessary things on credit.

Stupidity level: 6/10

Risk level: 1/10

David was tired of driving around in the old, reliable used car that he had owned since he was in driving school. At 18, fresh out of high school and eager for college, he decided to take a big step. He decided to buy a brand new car, a shiny model that had been in his dreams for years.

The loan amount for the car was a whopping $30,000 and he had chosen a loan term of 5 years with an interest rate of 5% per year. That meant he had to pay a loan payment of $500 a month. David's monthly payments consisted of interest of approximately $125 and principal of $375.

David's brand new car was undoubtedly an eye-catcher and was well received by the women in his neighborhood. His friends also admired his car and often asked for a spin.

The first few years went well for David. He had graduated and found a job. The monthly car payments were manageable and he enjoyed the ride in his dream car. But things gradually changed. He began piling up other financial obligations – rent, insurance, groceries and other bills.

In addition to the loan payment for his car, he also had to pay for repairs and maintenance as his dream car got older. Burst tires, broken brakes and expensive oil changes never seemed to end. David often found himself spending a significant portion of his already limited budget on car repairs. The constant financial stress and the fact that he hadn't paid off much of his car loan began to weigh heavily on his heart. David realized that he needed to take urgent action to get his financial situation under control and reduce his debt.

Andy was a smart and financially responsible young man. Instead of taking out a loan for an expensive new car, he set out to find a used vehicle that met his needs and was within his budget. He browsed the online advertisements for weeks and waited patiently for the perfect bargain.

Eventually he found a well-maintained, reliable used vehicle that met his needs. The seller asked for $5,000, and Andy was able to successfully bargain and purchase the car for 4000.

Over the next three years, Andy treated his car with care and performed regular maintenance. When the time came to part with the vehicle, he found a buyer willing to pay him $4,200 for the same car he had purchased. So Andy didn't make a loss and was able to use the money from the sale for his next car.

Andy's story is in stark contrast to David's story. While David struggled with an expensive car loan and had to deal with significant monthly payments and unforeseen expenses for repairs, Andy was able to act financially wisely. He put time and effort into finding an affordable used car and managed to get by with no debt and no loss.

Conclusion:

Loans are not inherently bad. However, you should think carefully about whether you want to be financially tied to your current purchase for the next few years. After a short time, the joy of a new car fades while the monthly burden remains.

Especially when multiple loans are involved, many young people have lost control and overview of their repayment rates, interest rates and total debts. They start their adult life with a lot of financial burden and find it difficult to get out of the debt trap. It's best to seek advice from experienced people you can trust before making any big financial decision that involves taking out a loan

9.)

Don't do crazy tricks on a trampoline!

Stupidity level: 4/10

Risk level: 7/10

Leo was a passionate trampolinist. There was an impressive trampoline in his garden, which gave him and his friends the opportunity to try out spectacular jumps and multiple somersaults. The summer was perfect for perfecting their skills and challenging each other.

One sunny day, Leo and his friends gathered in the garden. They had already thought of many breathtaking tricks, but today they wanted to do a double somersault. Leo was determined to master this trick and capture it on video.

They started by jumping on the trampoline and warming up. The friends cheered each other on to jump higher and more spectacularly. Leo had a clear plan: he would jump as high as possible and then do the double somersault. The tension rose.

Leo took a running start, jumped into the air with full force and successfully executed the first somersault. The spectators were impressed. But when he tried the second somersault, he got into a slight misalignment. His heart raced as he realized he was about to lose control of his body. Time seemed to stand still as he drifted headfirst off the trampoline.

With a loud thud, Leo landed on the ground next to the trampoline. The silence in the garden was broken by a painful scream.

Leo landed on his back with a loud thud and immediately sensed that something bad had happened. He suffered a serious spinal injury that would change his life forever. After an emergency operation and a long period of rehabilitation, Leo has been in a wheelchair ever since.

Leo and his friends underestimated the risks, and that had fatal consequences.

According to statistics from the US Consumer Product Safety Commission (CPSC), there were more than 333,000 emergency room visits due to trampoline accidents in 2020. These numbers illustrate the danger that trampoline jumping can pose, especially when done improperly.

Conclusion:

If you land on your head or back, this usually has fatal consequences. So don't do crazy tricks on a trampoline.

10.)

Why you shouldn't jump out of moving trains or cars.

Stupidity level: 7/10

Risk level: 7/10

Michael and his buddy Tom have always been known for their addiction to adrenaline. This time, however, they had an idea that was pretty daring even for them. It was a sunny Saturday afternoon when they decided to jump from a moving train into a river.

The two friends had chosen the train station as a meeting point and they found themselves on an abandoned platform. The train, a slow freight train, rolled leisurely in their direction. The friends went to the deserted end of the station and made sure no one was watching. Then the moment came. Michael grabbed the first carriage and pulled himself up, followed by Tom. When the train left a few minutes later, they laughed with excitement as the wind blew through their hair.

As the train rumbled over an old bridge that spanned a wide river, the friends prepared to make their risky leap. Michael was supposed to jump first while Tom filmed his jump and then followed. Tom waited for the right moment and took a running start to avoid landing on the nearby tracks. When he jumped, the train had just reached the beginning of the river. Tom followed right behind him. However, both had underestimated the power of train speed. Michael landed just at the other end of the river, and Tom hit a rocky ledge on the other side of the river with full force.

He was lucky and only broke one leg. However, the accident could have ended worse. He could even have died. Because what Michael and Tom hadn't considered was the distance and the offset trajectory.

When you jump from a moving train or car, various forces act on your body so that you don't land where you jumped out. Not even close. This behavior is best explained by the principles of inertia and relative motion. An object in motion tends to remain in motion unless external forces act on it. So when you jump out of a moving train, you take over the speed and direction of the train. So you continue moving at the same speed and direction as the train. The force of gravity ultimately pulls you downwards and accelerates your flight.

Conclusion:

If you jump out of moving trains or cars, you will most likely end up somewhere completely different than you think. So it's better not to do this.

11.)

Don't risk your life for a cool selfie.

Stupidity level: 10/10

Risk level: 10/10

Michael and Thomas have been best friends since childhood. They discovered a common passion early on that connected them closely: climbing. But not just any climbing - they sought out the tallest buildings and the most dangerous construction sites to put themselves in life-threatening situations and take breathtaking photos and videos for their Instagram channel.

Their channel, was no longer an insider tip. With thousands of followers, they were now known in the world of extreme athletes and daredevils. The two loved to put their skills to the test and impress again and again. But this time they had planned something special.

The location of their latest adventure was an imposing skyscraper that was being built in the center of the city. The scaffolding surrounded the building like a huge network of steel and iron. Michael and Thomas planned to climb the scaffolding at dusk and photograph the most spectacular sunset in the city from there.

The two friends sneaked up to the construction site in the darkness and skillfully climbed up the scaffolding. Her heart pounded with excitement as they climbed higher and higher. With each step they climbed, the view became more breathtaking. The city lights twinkled below them and the sky slowly turned into the warm colors of sunset. Finally they reached the highest platform of the scaffolding, which gave them a clear view of the entire city. Thomas pulled out his camera and began to capture the impressive scenery. Michael, on the other hand, becoming more and more courageous, thought about how he could take the most dangerous selfie of his life. He finally hung on the railing with both arms and looked down.

The depth beneath him was breathtaking. He could see the tiny people on the streets that looked like ants. The wind whistled around him and his adrenaline spiked.

Michael was only hanging on the railing by one arm and took his smartphone out of his pocket with the other hand. He slowly held his phone up in the air while gripping the railing with his other hand. The click of the self-timer was his signal to now fully concentrate on his target. His expression was both determined and excited as he took the dangerous selfie.

Thomas, who had the camera trained on Michael the entire time, couldn't hide his concern. But he trusted his friend and knew that they could both rely on their abilities.

The selfie was taken and Michael went to put his phone in his pocket when he couldn't grab his bag anymore. His long sweater had slipped over his pocket, making it difficult for him to store his cell phone. Since he was holding the phone in one happy hand, he couldn't use his fingers to push the sweater aside. Eventually his strength left him and he had to make the decision to let go of the phone and climb up or fall down with the phone. He dropped the phone and tried to grab hold of it with his other arm. But by now the action had exhausted him so much that he could no longer pull himself up on his own. Thomas couldn't help him because the railing he was on was too thin to support him and pull him up.

His strength had left him and he realized that he had found himself in a hopeless situation from which there was only one way out: falling. Thomas tried to find a solution, but he couldn't find a rope or other support option. "Hold on!" he shouted as he ran away to find a way to grab hold. After 4 minutes he returned with a steel bar that Michael could have held on to. But Michael was no longer there. He fell because he wanted to take an impressive selfie.

Conclusion:

On the Internet you only see the spectacular photos and videos, but you will never see the many accidents. The price of a cool selfie is higher than you think. Many paid with their own lives. So if such a thoughtless idea ever comes to mind, think of this text and find another hobby.

12.)

Stay away from the bowling pinsetter!

Stupidity level: 2/10

Risk level: 3/10

Thomas was out with his friends at the local bowling alley that Friday evening. They were celebrating his birthday and had already had a lot of fun. The atmosphere was exuberant and the drinks were flowing freely. Thomas had had a few too many beers and was feeling in good spirits. As he watched his friends knock over the pins, he had a stupid idea. He stared at the pinsetters at the end of the bowling alley and thought it would be a great idea to sneak over there and place the bowling ball before it was pushed back again. It seemed like a fun and harmless activity that would lighten the mood even further.

Thomas waited for the right moment when the bowling alley employees weren't looking. He crept quietly along the shiny track, swaying and reeling. Eventually he reached the pin setters, the huge, automatic machines that shuttled the bowling balls back to the players. Thomas chuckled to himself and began placing the bowling ball on the conveyor belt.

But he had completely underestimated the dangers of these machines. As he let go of the ball, it slipped from his drunken hand and landed on the conveyor belt. Before he could react, the ball was pulled rapidly into the darkness of the engine room. Thomas tried to grab it, but he lost his balance and fell headfirst into the engine room.

It was dark and loud in the narrow space dominated by the moving parts of the pin setters. Thomas could barely orientate himself and felt himself being pushed from one part to the next. He screamed in fear and pain as he tried to free himself. His friends and staff heard his screams, but it took some time before they realized what had happened.

Eventually, bowling alley employees managed to stop the machines. Thomas was rescued from the dangerous area with scratches and bruises, but he was lucky again. The Pin Setters are complex and dangerous machines that can be extremely dangerous to unprotected people. Thomas had completely underestimated their danger.

Conclusion:

Stay away from bowling pinsetters.

13.)

Why you shouldn't even start smoking.

Stupidity level: 2/10

Risk level: 5/10

Sam grew up in a small town where most of his friends spent their time after school at the local skateboard park. But he never had the same talent for skating as his friends. He often felt out of place and longed for a way to fit in better.

The history of Sam's initiation into smoking was marked by insecurity and a constant feeling of being different. His parents had divorced several years ago and he lived with his mother, who worked hard to support the family. The financial and emotional strain of the divorce had often left Sam feeling abandoned.

One day after school, as he was sitting at his favorite park watching his friends skate, he noticed his best friends, Max and Lisa, meeting a group of other teenagers in a corner of the park.

As he approached, he noticed that most of the group were smoking. When Max and Lisa offered him a cigarette, Sam hesitated but eventually lit it. The first hit was bitter and made him cough, but he didn't want to look like a coward. The others in the group seemed to enjoy smoking and pretended to feel relaxed.

Sam found that smoking was a common ritual among this group. They met after school, shared stories and laughed while smoking together. For a brief moment, he felt like he finally belonged. His insecurity and feeling of being different were forgotten for the moment.

Time passed and Sam joined his friends more and more often on their cigarette breaks. He didn't want to be the one standing outside while the others were having fun anymore. But he soon realized that he couldn't quit smoking as easily as he had originally thought. Cigarette breaks became a regular part of his daily routine, and he couldn't ignore the urges and withdrawal symptoms. He found himself caught in a gradual process that drew him deeper and deeper into the world of smoking and increasingly influenced his life. Since he turned 25, he sometimes made half-hearted attempts to quit smoking, but the addiction always overcame him.

The first signs of his poor decision were subtle, but gradually they became obvious. His skin began to age prematurely. By his mid-30s, Sam already had deep wrinkles around his eyes and mouth that his friends his age didn't yet have. His skin was losing its elasticity, and it seemed as if the cigarettes were digging into every wrinkle even deeper. Smoking also affected the blood flow to his skin, resulting in a pale complexion.

Another visible effect was the thinning and graying of his hair. By his mid-30s, Sam already had more gray hairs than he could count. His once full head of hair had become thin and lifeless, and he felt uncomfortable with it.

Although he regularly cared for his teeth, they became severely discolored and took on an unpleasant yellow hue. Smoking not only caused discoloration but also led to problems with his gums. He developed gum disease, which not only affected him aesthetically but also caused pain and discomfort.

However, the effects of smoking weren't just apparent on the surface. Growing up, Sam was an enthusiastic athlete who enjoyed jogging and playing football. But as time went on, his physical fitness became worse and worse. His lung capacity was impaired and he quickly became short of breath even during light physical activity. This led to him having to give up the sport he once loved.

Over the years, he developed serious health problems that went beyond the superficial effects of smoking. He developed chronic bronchitis, which led to constant coughing fits. His morning cough was excruciating, and he suffered from difficulty breathing, which significantly affected his daily life.

But the hardest blow came when he turned 50. During a medical examination he was diagnosed with lung cancer. Nicotine addiction had a tragic impact on his life. Suddenly he was no longer just battling the superficial effects of smoking, but a fatal illness.

Conclusion:

Smoking is directly linked to a variety of serious health problems. Tobacco smoke contains thousands of chemicals, many of which have been shown to be carcinogenic. Lung cancer is probably one of the most well-known consequences of smoking. It significantly increases the risk of lung cancer. In addition, smokers are also at a higher risk of other types of cancer, such as mouth, larynx and esophageal cancer.

In addition to cancer, cardiovascular diseases are also widespread among smokers. Smoking increases blood pressure and causes blood vessels to constrict, which dramatically increases the risk of heart attacks and strokes. Smoking impairs lung function and can lead to chronic respiratory diseases such as chronic obstructive pulmonary disease (COPD).

Smoking is also a major factor in the development of tooth and gum disease. It leads to bad breath, yellowing of teeth and, in severe cases, tooth loss. In addition, smoking negatively affects skin health and accelerates the aging process.

The financial impact of smoking is just as significant as the health impact. Cigarettes are expensive, and spending on tobacco products adds up significantly over time. Smokers not only spend money on cigarettes themselves, but also on health care costs related to smoking-related illnesses. Treatment for cancer, cardiovascular disease, and tooth and gum problems can be very costly.

Additionally, smokers often face higher life insurance premiums and even higher health insurance costs. Their lifestyle is viewed as riskier by insurance companies, resulting in higher premiums.

Since you, the reader of this book, are probably under 20 years old, it should be clear: the best way is not to start smoking in the first place. Smoking is only cool if you're a cowboy or James Bond. Since neither is true, you should stop immediately or not start at all.

14.)

Why you shouldn't climb on a pool cover.

Stupidity level: 5/10

Risk level: 7/10

Paul had spent the entire day preparing the pool in his backyard for the upcoming pool party. The sun was hot and he couldn't wait to invite his friends over and have a great time with them. Everything was perfectly prepared: the grill was ready, the music was playing softly in the background, and the pool glittered seductively in the sunlight.

But Paul was so excited that he didn't notice how he carelessly stepped on the fabric-like tarpaulin of the pool cover. He immediately sank into the pool along with the tarpaulin. The tarp collapsed on him and the water closed over his head.

The darkness and the confines of the tarp surrounded Paul and he didn't have time to take a breath. Panic seized him and he began to flail wildly to get to the surface, but the tarp kept him more and more trapped. With each additional movement, the tarp became further tangled around him, trapping him underwater.

His friends heard the noise, noticed his muffled scream and the wildly splashing water, but they couldn't immediately tell what had happened. When they finally noticed that Paul was missing and the pool cover had collapsed, they understood the danger.

One of the bravest friends jumped into the pool and felt his way under the tarp. The darkness and weight of the tarp made the rescue difficult, but he eventually found Paul, tangled in the cover and unable to free himself. The friend fought against the rising panic and was finally able to free Paul and bring him to the surface.

Paul coughed and gasped for air, but fortunately was unhurt. The party ended abruptly and everyone was shocked by what had happened. Paul had narrowly escaped death, and it was an important lesson for everyone present about how dangerous careless behavior could be.

Conclusion:

Pool covers are death traps. They are designed to float on the water, increasing the likelihood that the material will likely be pulled close to you by the buoyancy of the rest of the cover. Once you're trapped in the tarp, any further movement will entangle you further. So give them a wide berth.

15.)

Why you should never put your feet up as a passenger.

Stupidity level: 1/10

Risk level: 3/10

Oliver was a young man who loved adventure. Whether it was traveling, outdoor activities or just exploring new places, he was always ready to embark on new adventures. One sunny Saturday morning, his friend Max invited him on a spontaneous road trip, and Oliver didn't hesitate to accept.

The two friends set off in Max's old but trusty car. The streets were clear, the sun was shining, and the music was playing loudly from the speakers. The atmosphere was relaxed and Oliver could literally feel the anticipation for the weekend. But he had a bad habit: he loved to rest his legs on the car dashboard when he sat in the passenger seat.

The dashboard felt nice and cool, and Oliver relaxed by resting his legs on it. He enjoyed the comfort and thought it was a great way to relax during the long drive. Max was driving at high speed on the highway and they were laughing and talking, unaware of the danger that lay ahead.

Suddenly, without warning, the unthinkable happened. The car in front of them braked abruptly as an animal crossed the street. Max only had a moment to react, and he successfully applied the brakes in time to avoid a major disaster. Nonetheless, there was a collision in which both vehicles bumped into each other at a moderate speed. Thankfully, the reduced speed prevented the cars from being completely destroyed.

Unfortunately, Oliver, whose legs were still on the dashboard, had no luck. The airbag deployed with a loud bang, and the sudden pressure pushed Oliver's legs, who had been propping them up on the dashboard, backwards. The pressure was so brutal that his legs suffered a grotesque deformation from his knees to his feet. His knees were pushed forward and his thigh bones, which normally run straight, were now bent at an unnatural angle. The shins and calf bones had also suffered severe damage. The consequences of this terrible accident were devastating. Oliver's legs were badly injured, the muscles and ligaments were torn, and the bones had suffered multiple fractures. The injuries were so severe that Oliver immediately went into shock and screamed in pain when emergency responders arrived at the scene.

Doctors at the hospital determined that Oliver needed extensive surgery to stabilize his legs. Multiple surgeries were required to fix the broken bones with metal plates and screws. The muscles and ligaments required reconstruction, and it was uncertain whether Oliver would ever be able to walk without walking aids again. The damage to Oliver's legs was not only physically devastating, but also emotionally devastating. He had to undergo months of intensive rehabilitation to be able to walk again and lead a somewhat normal life. The experience left deep scars, both physical and psychological.

Conclusion:

Even at lower speeds, resting your feet on the dashboard as a passenger can result in knee-to-pelvis impact in the event of a sudden stop or collision. Even if it's not that comfortable, always sit properly in a car.

16.)

Always have the headrest behind your head in the car.

Stupidity level: 1/10

Risk level: 3/10

It goes without saying that you should also wear a seatbelt in a car. This book will therefore not discuss this separately. However, many people are not aware of how important it is to adjust the headrest to the correct height. This is particularly crucial if you are a passenger in someone else's car, as the headrest may not be optimally aligned with you.

Why does this matter? If the car is involved in an accident, your body immediately begins to move forward as the seatback pushes you in that direction. However, if nothing supports your head region, it will lag until the movement of your body eventually pulls it along. Given enough speed, this can cause a separation between the base of the skull and the spine. The only barrier that protects your head in this situation is the elasticity of the skin. Likewise, your head can suddenly buckle if someone rear-ends you. However, the thing with the headrests is not always that easy, especially if you are a tall. Some cars simply don't allow you to adjust the headrests high enough. In this case, you should look for an individual adjustment or a new car. At least drive extra carefully.

Conclusion:

Always have the headrest behind your head in the car.

17.)

Always put your smartphone in the glove box when driving.

Stupidity level: 7/10
Risk level: 8/10

Niclas, a 32-year-old computer scientist, had turned his morning commute into a boring routine. The commute usually took about 45 minutes, and he spent most of that time on his smartphone. He had long been aware that he had developed an addiction. He usually couldn't even go five minutes while driving without looking at his cell phone.

Over time, he lost awareness of the real world around him. He crossed intersections, overtook other cars and drove past traffic jams without really noticing. Once, when he almost missed the end of a traffic jam, he was briefly startled and put his cell phone aside for a moment. But the unpleasant feeling of boredom and the longing for new stimuli quickly drove him back into the digital world.

On that fateful morning, while Niclas was driving on the highway, he was particularly engrossed in a WhatsApp group. The excitement of responding to messages and engaging in interesting conversations had completely captivated him. He was so immersed in the world of news that he didn't notice the brake lights in front of him.

When the cars in front of him braked abruptly, it was too late. Niclas crashed into the rear of the vehicle in front of him with full force. The airbags deployed, metal crunched, and the impact was so violent that Niclas lost consciousness.

When he slowly came to, he found himself in a hospital bed. But something wasn't right. He tried to move, but his body wouldn't obey him. The pain shot through his body and he could only turn his head with difficulty. A doctor stood next to him and explained to him the severity of the accident. Niclas suffered a concussion, bruises and broken bones. But that wasn't the worst of it.

Reality slowly began to sink in, and Niclas couldn't believe what he was hearing. The doctor told him that he was paraplegic. He could not believe it. It felt like he was trapped in a nightmare. He tried to move, but his body didn't respond. The realization hit him like a blow.

"You were very lucky," said the doctor as she announced the bitter truth. "The accident could have ended much worse. Your spine was severely damaged and I'm sorry to inform you that you are now a paraplegic. Niclas still couldn't believe it. His life felt like a cruel one Dream from which he could not wake up. Now he was faced with the grave consequences of his carelessness, and the harsh reality had crept into his life."

He would never be able to walk again.

But it got worse.

The car he hit belonged to a young family on their way to a weekend getaway. The parents died instantly and the small child in the car suffered serious injuries. Niclas felt as if he had unleashed an avalanche of misery.

As he listened to the news, which settled in his mind like an evil curse, he realized that he had irretrievably destroyed not only his own life, but also the lives of others. The guilt overwhelmed him and he could hardly believe the tragedy he had caused.

In addition to the severe physical and emotional stress, Niclas also had to bear legal consequences. The police investigated negligent homicide and endangering life. He was facing a long prison sentence, and he understood that he would be trapped in a nightmare for the rest of his life. His career had become distant, his future was uncertain, and the life he had once known was now in ruins. Niclas' family and friends were shocked and didn't know how to deal with him. His once carefree life had turned into a nightmare.

Conclusion:

If you don't consciously break the habit, looking at your smartphone while driving will one day become a habit. You'll look at it multiple times during each ride and maybe even type or send voicemails at the same time. To prevent this from happening, it's crucial that you act now and consistently put your smartphone in the glove compartment, even if your trip is short. This action should become as routine as putting on a seatbelt."

18.)

Why you should never go near small dams or rapids.

Stupidity level: 2/10

Risk level: 8/10

Andy was an adventurous young man who loved nature. On a sunny Saturday morning, he decided to grab his kayak and take a trip on a nearby river. The river was lined with dense forest and the gentle current promised a relaxing paddling experience. But what Andy didn't know was that there was a small dam with dangerous rapids just downstream.

Andy climbed into the sparkling water in his canoe and enjoyed the peace and quiet of nature. The gentle rippling of the water and the chirping of the birds accompanied him on his journey. As he neared the dam he could hear a faint rushing sound, but he thought it was just the current changing slightly.

Unprepared, Andy approached the dam when the canoe was suddenly caught in the current. He fought to maintain control, but it was too late. The kayak was dragged near the dangerous rapids and eventually capsized. Andy was thrown into the deep end.

Panic overtook him as he tried to get back to the surface. However, the masses of water kept pulling him down, and the pressure in this part of the river made it almost impossible to get up. Andy struggled desperately, fighting for air as he was pulled deeper into the dark depths of the river.

The seconds felt like hours as he fought against the relentless pull of the water. His heart was racing with fear and his lungs were screaming for air. But then, when he had almost given up hope, he managed to fight his way to the surface with one last desperate push.

With the last of his strength he pulled himself to the edge of the river and held on. His body shook with exhaustion and cold, and water dripped from his face. He had survived. The danger wasn't over yet as the kayak was swept away by the rapids, but Andy was saved.

Dams are built to store water for various reasons. But there are dangers both above and below dams. The water passes over the dam and then falls, creating a dangerous backwash. This current can suck in boats and people and become very dangerous. When someone is caught in this current, they are drawn to the dam surface and then pushed downstream until they reach the "boiling point," where the water comes to the surface from below and moves either downstream or back toward the dam. This dangerous cycle repeats itself.

Complicating matters further is that dams are often covered with debris such as tires and logs on the surface and rocks and steel rods underneath, increasing the risk of becoming trapped.

The depth of the dam is not a determining factor in the danger. During floods and heavy rain, backwash becomes even more dangerous and extends further downstream.

Small, low-waterfall dams that seem safe when water levels are low can be deadly when river levels rise. In short, it is not the collapse of the dam that is dangerous, but the backwash, which depends on the volume and speed of water.

Conclusion:

The danger below the dam is often only recognized when it is too late. Shallow dams are difficult to see upstream. In most cases they look harmless, but can be life-threatening. Therefore, always pay attention to warning signs, markings or buoys and avoid shallow dams.

19.)

Why you shouldn't listen to music loudly.

Stupidity level: 2/10
Risk level: 3/10

Achim had a passionate love for music. Every day, as soon as he put on his headphones, he was immersed in a world of sounds and rhythms. But Achim had a habit that would soon develop into a serious problem: He would often turn the music way too loud to be able to hear it over the deafening noise of cars in the city on the way to work or while jogging.

At first, listening to loud music seemed harmless. Achim enjoyed the beats and melodies at full volume and felt like he could best experience the music that way. But what he didn't realize was that he was doing a lot of damage to his ears.

Over time, he began to notice the first signs of his hearing impairment. He increasingly had to ask questions when someone spoke to him because he could no longer understand the words clearly. The quiet sounds of everyday life were lost in an indistinct murmur, and even the ringing of his alarm clock in the morning seemed to reach him only faintly.

But instead of taking care of his health and reducing the volume, Achim just carried on. He rejected the well-intentioned advice of his friends and family and buried himself deeper and deeper in his loud music.

The effects of his negligence became increasingly clear. Achim not only lost his joy in everyday noises, but also in social activities. Meeting friends in noisy restaurants or bars became torture for him because he could hardly follow the conversations. His work also suffered as he often missed important information in meetings.

Finally, Achim visited an ENT doctor when he noticed that his hearing had decreased dramatically. The doctor examined his ears and determined that Achim had suffered permanent hearing loss. The small hair cells in his inner ears had been irreparably damaged by listening to loud music. Achim had taken his own hearing.

Hearing damage can be irreversible in many cases, especially when caused by excessive noise or loud music. This is because the inner ear contains delicate hair cells that can be damaged by excessive noise or loud sound levels. These hair cells are crucial for converting sound into electrical signals that are transmitted to the brain, and once damaged they typically cannot be restored.

Achim was shocked and sad about the diagnosis. He realized that his reckless behavior now had far-reaching consequences for his life. He had to equip himself with hearing aids in order to be able to participate to some extent in social life. The simple joy of music that had once filled his life was now just a fading memory for him.

Conclusion:

Don't listen to music too loudly with headphones, your ears will thank you!

20.)
Never fall asleep outside drunk in winter!

Stupidity level: 5/10
Risk level: 9/10

Björn came from the small town of Eksjö in Sweden, where winters could be particularly cold. That evening he had decided to leave the confines of the small town for a party in the nearby town. His friend Erik invited him and promised that it would be an unforgettable night.

The party was in full swing when Björn arrived. There was loud music, happy people and plenty of alcohol. Björn, who was normally a level-headed person, got carried away by the exuberant atmosphere and drank more than he intended. The hours flew by and the effects of the alcohol became stronger and stronger.

Around midnight, Björn decided it was time to leave the party. The alcohol level in his blood was alarmingly high and he no longer wanted to drink. He realized that his speech was reduced to a slurred, incomprehensible mumble, and focusing his eyes to see straight ahead became an arduous task. With a pang of realization and a wave of self-disgust, he admitted to himself that he was in no condition to be out in public and headed home.

But the icy winter night wasn't the best time to be out alone, especially in his condition. The alcohol impaired his coordination and he staggered down the street. When he finally arrived at his front door, he looked for his keys, but they seemed to be missing.

His senses were dulled and his fingertips were so numb with cold that he couldn't feel the keys in his pockets. He searched his jacket and trouser pockets several times, but to no avail.

His keys!

Panic struck him as he searched for them in his pockets. They were gone! Maybe he had lost her somewhere in the euphoria of the party. He desperately tried to force the door open, but his frosty fingers prevented him from doing so.

Completely exhausted from the cold and the alcohol, Björn decided to lie down on the porch and take a short nap.

"Just for a few minutes," he thought, "then I'll wake up and find a solution." But the alcohol and the cold had already taken hold of him.

In this terrible situation, Björn was lucky in misfortune. A neighbor walking his dog early in the morning found him and immediately called the ambulance. The rescue workers arrived quickly and took Björn to the hospital.

The doctors fought for hours to save Björn's life. His body was severely damaged by frostbite. They had to amputate parts of his fingers and toes to save his life.

After this incident, Björn had to completely reorganize his life. He was no longer able to work like he used to and required intensive rehabilitation to adapt to his new physical limitations. The party that promised so much fun had changed his life forever.

Björn's story served as a warning to others. She reminded people how dangerous alcohol abuse combined with freezing cold can be. It was a miracle that he survived, but he paid a heavy price for his carelessness.

Conclusion:

Never lie down drunk outside somewhere in winter to rest or even sleep. The cold will freeze you in your sleep without you even realizing it. You will simply fall asleep and never wake up again. If you ever find yourself in a situation like this, make every effort to seek warmth or, at the very least, stay awake until sunrise and bask in the sun.

21.)

Why you shouldn't drink a whole bottle of hard alcohol in one go.

Stupidity level: 8/10
Risk level: 9/10

William was a young man who often felt the need to prove himself and look good in front of his friends. One evening, as was often the case, he was invited to a party. After some drinks, he became more and more reckless and, after a few drinking games, decided to make a stupid and disastrous bet: He believed he could drink a whole bottle of vodka in one go

In the past, William had always proven that he was a heavy drinker. While his friends caved, he maintained relative control. Due to his height of 6.5 ft (2 meters) and his weight of 242 lbs (110 kilograms), he tolerated alcohol better than his lighter friends.

But he had never drunk an entire bottle in one go. He chose a 1 liter Absolut Vodka bottle that was still sealed.

This was important because it meant he could prove via video that it was real vodka and not bottled water. The surrounding partygoers gathered around him and the cameras were rolling. And action:

He opened the cap with a click and brought the neck of the bottle to his mouth. He drained the bottle in a minute without putting it down once. Shortly after completing his glorious act, he didn't notice much except the cheers of the other partygoers. But soon after, things began to spiral out of control.

He lost the ability to think clearly after just a few minutes. His coordination was severely impaired and he began knocking over things and stumbling. His friends, who had initially laughed, became concerned. Eventually he reached a point where he couldn't even slur and fell to the ground, unconscious. His friends called an ambulance and William was taken to the hospital. There, doctors diagnosed life-threatening alcohol poisoning.

In a 1 liter bottle of Absolut Vodka the alcohol content is 40%. Arnold had consumed 0.4 liters of pure alcohol in a very short time. For comparison: a 0.3 liter bottle of beer with 5% alcohol contains only 15 milliliters of pure alcohol.

After ingestion, the alcohol enters the bloodstream via the lining of the stomach and small intestine and is largely broken down in the liver. In the body, the alcohol molecule produces carbon dioxide and water. These are the final breakdown products of alcohol - the carbon dioxide is excreted through the lungs and the water passes into the body's cells.

However, in the case of alcohol poisoning, there is too much ethanol in the organism and cannot be broken down. Blood alcohol concentration is measured in per mille, which means how many milligrams of pure alcohol are present in one gram (approximately one milliliter) of blood. On average, the liver can reduce blood alcohol levels by 0.1 to 0.2 per mille per hour. So only a limited amount of alcohol can be broken down per hour. If the amount of alcohol consumed exceeds this rate of breakdown, the alcohol concentration in the blood increases.

High levels of alcohol in the blood have a toxic effect on the central nervous system, which can cause symptoms such as loss of consciousness, confusion, seizures and breathing problems. Alcohol poisoning can also affect other vital organs such as the heart, kidneys, and liver, leading to organ failure.

If an unconscious person is admitted to a hospital with alcohol poisoning, doctors monitor important body functions such as heartbeat, breathing and circulation. In most cases, a so-called full electrolyte solution helps to replenish fluid and lost electrolytes into the body. A 24-hour stay in the hospital is often enough to treat the poisoning. In particularly severe cases, the treatment time is extended, for example if the patient falls into a coma or the organs have suffered severe damage. After his release from the hospital, William will struggle with a severe hangover for the next few days. He was lucky because his heavy weight meant he was able to spread the alcohol over a large crowd, he had eaten a lot in the evening and his friends quickly called an ambulance. Many people have already died from much smaller amounts of alcohol.

Conclusion:

Always drink carefully. The action of drinking an entire bottle in one go is life-threatening. Even if you don't get severe alcohol poisoning, the party will definitely be over for you since you won't be able to do anything except embarrass yourself in front of everyone.

22.)

Why you should never put New Year's Eve firecrackers in your mouth.

Stupidity level: 7/10

Risk level: 7/10

It was midnight and Nic's New Year's Eve party was in full swing. The guests cheered and congratulated each other on the New Year. The atmosphere was exuberant and the drinks were flowing freely.

As the countdown to the New Year began and the clock finally struck 12 midnight, partygoers toasted each other. Champagne splashed into the air and friends hugged each other warmly. The night promised to be unforgettable.

While most people continued partying inside, Lukas and his friends retreated outside. There they took a few more shots and fired firecrackers, which exploded brightly in the night sky. The loud bangs and colorful lights blended seamlessly into the festive atmosphere.

At the same time, selfies were taken in abundance. The guests wanted to capture every moment of this special evening. Lukas, who was standing outside smoking and enjoying the smoke from the fireworks in the air, suddenly came up with a brilliant idea. "Why not take a cool picture?" he thought to himself, "smoke a New Year's Eve firecracker instead of a cigarette?" The idea fascinated him and he felt the adrenaline rush.

Without hesitating for long, Lukas reached into his pocket and pulled out one of the remaining firecrackers. His friends laughed and encouraged him. They took out their cell phones to capture the moment forever. Lukas put the firecracker in his mouth and lit it. Then suddenly: BOOM! Just as he was about to throw the firecracker away, there was a loud bang and a loud screech drowned out the party music.

The fuse was shorter than expected. Lukas had lost his entire lower jaw. The teeth, bones and blood were blasted in all directions within a millisecond. His jaw was just a piece of shredded skin with a piece that used to be a tongue. The guests could see directly into his open neck. Lukas himself, still in shock, only realized from the looks of the frightened party guests and the blood that was everywhere that something was wrong about this situation. He had no pain from the shock; When he realized what had happened, he couldn't believe it. Why had he done such a reckless thing? He fainted shortly afterwards and an ambulance was called.

Lukas was saved and survived the accident, although he lost a lot of blood. Only two of his teeth remained intact, and he underwent an artificial jaw prosthesis and several facial surgeries over a period of two years. This process was accompanied by severe pain and consisted mainly of operations to heal and prepare for the next operation. Eating is still painful for him to this day, even though he now has artificial teeth. With a piece of his tongue torn off, he finds it difficult to speak clearly and his sense of taste is severely affected as he is missing the front part of his tongue.

Every day, Luke deeply regrets his actions. If only he had acted differently in that one brief moment, his life would have been completely different and better.

Conclusion:

Never put a firecracker in your mouth or smoke while throwing firecrackers at the same time. Such an accident can happen not only while taking photos, but also accidentally if you mistake a cigarette for a firecracker. It has already happened to many people.

23.)

Don't ruin your Life!

Every single situation I have talked about in this book has been experienced several times before and, unfortunately, will continue to happen. It is a sad truth that some mistakes are repeated, some risks are taken again. But in the midst of these repetitions lies the opportunity to act wiser and learn from the mistakes of others.

At the core of all of these situations is the realization that it is almost never worth taking enormous risks for a short-lived, seemingly funny moment.

It's easy to get carried away by the euphoria of the moment, but it takes great inner strength and wisdom to resist the impulse.

Make sure to protect not only yourself, but also your friends from rash and dangerous situations. It may sometimes seem like friendship to slide into unwise decisions together. But the truth is that true friendship comes from protecting each other from potential harm. If you're ever tempted to do something crazy, remember the stories told here, and you'll get through the next few years safe and perhaps even unscathed. It will not only save your life but also your parents' sanity.

Thank you for reading.

Even though this book is certainly not a literary masterpiece, there is a lot of work put into it. I really appreciate every single positive review on Amazon and will definitely read every single review. Your feedback might help other reckless risk-lovers benefit from the book's wisdom. With that in mind: take care of yourself and don't ruin your life.

Printed in Great Britain
by Amazon